Distractions
That Hinder You
From
Your Blessings

By

Tiffany Bostic

Distractions
That Hinder You
From
Your Blessings

By

Tiffany Bostic

Printed in the United States of America

Cover Design: BVS Designs
Editor: LPW Editing & Consulting Services

First Printing, 2017

ISBN-13: 978-1979634601

ISBN-10: 1979634602

CONTENTS

Acknowledgements

First and foremost, I give all the honor and glory to God. Thank You, Jesus for giving me the vision and title to this book. Thank You for giving me the insight to incorporate Your Holy Scriptures throughout the manuscript to minister to young women.

To my Spiritual Mother, Carolyn James, thank you for loving me and pouring into me. Most of all, thank you for believing in me.

To my kids, Jhmyra, Saaniya, and Kennedy; I thank God for all three of you. I'm honored that God has chosen me to be your mother.

Sibyl, you are a bright light in my life. It brightens my heart to be able to talk to you daily. Thanks for believing in me and supporting me. Love you.

To Sgt. Major Jones, thank you for encouraging me to birth my vision and pushing me every day to have two to three chapters written in my book. Grateful to be blessed with a sponsor to push me to greatness and believe in my abilities and my dreams.

To all of my followers and those who have supported me, thank you for your love and encouragement. Each of you play an intricate part in helping me pursue my goals.

Introduction

Being distracted from the plan of God is extremely dangerous. As a Christian I believe that God is the navigation of my life. When you start losing sight of God, you start trying to navigate your own life. Not only does this lead you the wrong way, but it can lead you in the direction of trial, sin, missed opportunities, and missed blessings. As we continue to live being distracted from God becomes easier. Being distracted is not always because of sin. Caught up in the world and wanting to be like everyone else is mainly why. TV, hobbies, money relationships, cell phones are good examples of being distracted. The more I focused on myself the more distracted I became from being on the right path. In this book I want to share with you my experiences of distractions that hindered me from my career and blessing.

No temptation has overtaken you that is usual for human beings. But God is faithful, and he will not allow you to be tempted beyond your strength. Instead, along with the temptation, he will also provide a way out, so that you may be able to endure it.

1 Corinthians 10:13

Chapter 1

The Distraction of a Friend

I anticipated the day of being able to make my own money. I had a plan that by my junior year of high school I would be driving a 1998 silver Nissan Altima with 18-inch rims. I have always wanted the best of everything and held the personality of an outgoing, strong minded, and goal-oriented young lady. So, I applied for a front-line position at Golden Corral and got hired on the same day. There was a lot of work involved but I didn't care; I wanted to make money to save for my own car. One day I was stocking cups at work and met a sweet young lady named April.

One day at work while sitting down taking a break, April approached me with some disturbing news. She needed a new place to live. She had a boyfriend, but he lived on the military base. April and I were so close that I was willing to ask my mom if she could live with us. When I got home from school, my mom was sitting in her favorite chair in the kitchen eating watermelon; so, I knew she was in a good mood. I told her about April's situation, and I asked her if April could live with us. My mom began to contemplate, but then she realized how much I cared about April and she agreed.

A week after moving in, April stated to me that her boyfriend had a roommate who was cute. I told myself that I didn't want a boyfriend; I wanted to stay focused on school and saving money. But convincingly, my friend said, "You can have fun together!" So, I began to ponder. I still didn't want any distractions in my life. I wanted to remain focused on my goals. But later, I decided to meet this guy. After a few phone conversations, car rides from school, ice cream stops and picking me up from work, I decided a friend wouldn't be a bad idea after all.

Eventually, my new boyfriend became adamant about me knowing where he lived. When I finally did go to his house, of course the tour included his bedroom. As we were walking to his room, he asked, "How far have you been with a guy?" I ignored the question and asked, "Please, can we go now?"

"Hold on a minute," he said, pulling me towards him. He was trying to kiss and feel on my body and I was very uncomfortable. He began trying to take my clothes off and the more I resisted, the harder he tried. Suddenly, I saw a black spot flash over my eyes after trying to stop him. My innocence was taken!

The next day, I was quiet and unhappy about how the night ended. A few months went by and I was still seeing my friend. The dates slowed down, phone conversations became very short, but the trips to Ft. Benning remained consistent. I found myself calling off work, leaving work early and giving shifts away to be with him. Even though I didn't want to continue a sexual relationship with my friend, my flesh was now out of control.

After the sixth month, I missed my period; surely my mind was playing games with me, and I thought to myself, "It will come soon." After school one day, I told my mom I had detention, so I could go to the local teen pregnancy center. Waiting patiently to be called, I was nervous and sweating. "Tiffany Bostic," the lady called tapping the pen on the clip board. "I need a urine sample," she said in a rude voice. With my head in my lap, I heard the door open and the words said nonchalantly, "You're pregnant."

A week went by and I had not said a word about anything; not even to April or my friend. I noticed I was more tired than usual, frequent trips to the bathroom and very bad headaches. What an awful way to feel! "I won't be able to get a car, neither will I be able to go to college. But more importantly, mom will be so disappointed," I thought.

Wednesday afternoon I rode the bus home instead of my friend picking me up. I got home, and noticed my mom was home too. "Why didn't your friend bring you home?" she asked.

As I ran upstairs, I softly replied, "I wanted to come on the bus." But as I began to undress, my mom walked right through the door and into my room. "Your breasts are getting big," she said. But I didn't say a word. "Tiffany, is there something you need to tell me? Are you pregnant?" she asked. My eyes looked as if I had seen a ghost. I couldn't say anything, so I just nodded my head.

It was dinner time and I didn't want to eat; I was exhausted. I was sleeping so good that I didn't hear April come in the room. The next morning, April asked, "Are you okay?" Shaking my head, my eyes filled up with water. "April, I'm pregnant!"

"Oh no!" "Did you tell your friend?" she asked. "No; and honestly, I really don't want to. He will probably want nothing to do with me." He was so adamant about not having kids. Oftentimes, he would make me drink vinegar after sex. I didn't ask why; I just did it.

The next day at work, I called my friend to pick me up so we could talk and he agreed. Thinking to myself, I wondered, "How do I tell him this news?" When he arrived, I could tell he had been drinking so I knew this would be a long evening. While we were walking to his room, he was feeling on me, trying to put his hands in my pants and kissing on me. The smell of the alcohol was a complete turn off and I didn't like it. Quickly, I said to him, "I have something to tell you."

Shouting at me, he said, "You better not be pregnant! If you are, stand up against the wall and let me kick you in the stomach."

I was in total disbelief! "What? Heck no! Take me home!"

"You're not going anywhere until I say so," he said. He kept trying to be abusive, but I kept threatening to tell on him. He tried to hit me, grabbing me by the neck, smashing my stomach, and forcing me to have more sex. He was completely out of control! Finally, he stopped.

During the ride back home, he tried to convince me to get an abortion. I agreed to all his suggestions, just so I could get home safely. I walked in the house and my mom was sitting in the kitchen with her close friend of the family. I could tell she was discerning something about me. As she began to speak, I began to cry. I confessed being pregnant. When April came home, she helped me decide the best solution for my situation. I concluded to go through with the pregnancy and never speak to my friend again.

Before I went to bed, I wrote in my diary about my plans. I had it all mapped out. I would graduate, have the baby, and then go to the technical college for a year. Afterwards, I would enlist into the Air Force. My mom agreed to help with the baby. Finally, I felt a relief and began to feel independent again.

 Soon thereafter, I woke up in the middle of the night because my stomach was hurting. I went to the hospital and they notified me that I was having a miscarriage. Truthfully, I was happy again and felt like I had my life back. April moved out and I never talked to her or my boyfriend again.

Have Mercy on me, my God, have mercy on me, for in you I take refuge. I will take refuge in the shadow of your wings until the disaster has passed.

Psalm 57:1 (NIV)

Chapter 2

The Distraction of my Senior Year

*F*our months left until graduation and I was overwhelmed, yet filled with excitement! I had plans to take the ASVAB test to get into the Air Force. After school one day, as I was walking from the mailbox, a black car backed all the way up and someone from inside the car yelled, "Excuse me!" "Yes?!" I answered. And the conversation took off.

"What's your name?" he yelled.

"Why do you want to know?"

"You look nice."

"Thank you," I replied. "I'm Tiffany," I said smiling.

"Here is my number; call me sometimes," he said. Then he drove off.

One night my friend Meka and I decided to go to a party. My mom was okay with me going as long as I was home by 11:00PM. I used Meka's cell phone to call my new friend. Ironically, his cousin lived right by the party we were attending. I asked him to come pick me up and he did. We went back to his house, went inside and began to talk. My friend respected my curfew and I made it home just in time.

To prepare myself for basic training, I began running in the neighborhood. I thought I was trying to get in shape. But the more I went running, the more I would visit my friend. One day I was having a bad day and I wanted to see my friend. We went to a park and I started discussing how I was having second thoughts about the enlisting. We started to make out and we both wanted each other. I trusted that everything would be okay and continued. Afterwards, something didn't seem right and I felt like I had made the wrong decision.

The rest of the evening, I remained quiet. I was never quiet around my new friend. I assumed it was just my emotions and that the feelings would pass. The next day at school, I was called to the senior counselor's office and was informed that I was two credits short from graduating. I was so nervous and afraid that I would not graduate! On the bus ride home from school, I was wondering, "What am I going to do?" Well, I had no choice but to tell my mom. After our conversation, we decided that I should enroll into a private school.

The next day, my mom and I went to visit the campus. It was so nice and less stressful than public school. One day in my English class, I started to feel very light headed. Therefore, I went to the break room to get a snack, but I still didn't feel better. This was a familiar feeling, so I started to become worried. I had one of my friends to pick me up, because I wanted to go see him. We stopped by the store first and I purchased a pregnancy test. I walked out with my head down; I was pregnant again.

We got back to my friend's house and I gave him the news. He wasn't upset at all, but I was disappointed in myself. I couldn't believe I had allowed this to happen again. I knew there was something wrong because we always used protection, except maybe once. I pondered, "How am I going to explain this?" This time, I wanted to tell my mother before she suspected anything. I decided to tell her on the way home from church. Her reaction was different this time. "How could you do this again Tiffany!" she yelled, slamming the car door.

When I went to the doctor, I was told that I was five months pregnant with a baby girl; but I wasn't showing at all. I was determined to be independent and graduate with my class, so I found a job working as a cashier at Winn-Dixie. I wanted to make sure that I had everything for my child. And any days I had off from the grocery store, I worked at Blockbuster Video. I wanted to prove to my mother that I was going to be a very responsible parent.

My due date was March 10, 2001. The closer I got to my due date, I became excited, yet nervous. On March 13, 2001, I gave birth to a healthy baby girl and named her Jhmyra Lanae Works. Two weeks after giving birth, I immediately went back to school. On June 7th, I graduated with my class, the same year that I would have graduated from Hardaway High School. I was so happy that my dream had come true.

Jhmyra's father and I got along really well for the most part. His mom would come in town and bring things for Jhmyra, but she wasn't really involved in her life. One day, Jhmyra and I went over to her father's house for a visit. He had been acting strange, but I didn't pay it any attention. I went to turn on the television and noticed a card from a family law firm on his stereo. I looked around to make sure he wasn't looking and I put the card in my pocket.

I rushed home to show my mother. We agreed that he was plotting something against me with our daughter. I felt betrayed and confronted him about the card. Yet, he assured there was nothing to worry about. But, my heart was not at peace about his answer.

Two years went by and I started to wonder why Jhmyra's dad didn't want to be more serious. At this point, I wanted more of a commitment. I was in college, I had my own place and my own car. Jhmyra's dad was always at my house; it was like we were living together. I would cook for him, wash and iron his clothes. I was getting fed up playing the role of a wife, but still had no ring on my finger. I felt it was time to give him an ultimatum.

One day, there was a knock on the door. "Who is it?" I asked. "Detective," he replied through the door. Slowly, I opened the door; he handed me a folded document and walked away. I grabbed Jhmyra and rushed to my mom's house. I showed her the document and we both were upset. Immediately, we called for an explanation. Jhmyra's father promised it was nothing; he said he wanted to put himself on child support so he could take care of his baby.

"Why?" I asked. "But we are together." He just kept saying, "Don't worry; it's nothing to be concerned about." I didn't believe him because I was discerning something different.

November came and it was my birthday. My boyfriend asked, "What do you want for your birthday?" My response was for us to live in a household together and have a stronger commitment. He became very quiet because I was giving him an ultimatum. I said, "If you can't commit to me, then we can't have sex anymore and you can't come over here unless you're visiting Jhmyra." He was livid, but I didn't care how he felt. He was up to something and I wanted the truth. He agreed to what I wanted, so we made plans to move in together.

The day came for us to find a place, and we found a townhouse that we both liked. But he sounded very weird on the phone. I met him at his place and he looked very suspicious. "What's wrong?" I asked.

"I'm not ready to move yet," he said.

"Why?" I asked.

"You did not give my daughter my last name at birth," he stated.

"Are you serious? You know my mom threatened to put me out of her house if I did that; you said you understood," I pleaded. "Why are you just bringing that up?" I asked crying. "You're trying to get out of moving! Forget it, I'm done with you. You knew exactly what you were doing. You just told me what I wanted to hear so you could keep using me. Stay away from me and my baby. You make me sick!" I screamed.

Right then and there, I made the decision to break up with him. I was hard because I really cared about him. He was already on child support, so I didn't have to worry about financial support for Jhmyra. I moved on with my life and he was not in the picture with exceptions of visitation.

Now I beseech you brethren, mark them which causes divisions and offences contrary to the doctrine which ye have learned; and avoid them.

Romans 16:17-18 (KJV)

Chapter 3

Distraction of Another Woman's Man

*A*fter my bad experiences with the last two boyfriends, I decided that I was just going to enjoy life for a while. I missed a lot of fun days with my friends because I became a parent right after graduation. I became close with my neighbor across the hall, Ms. Darlene. Her heart melted the day she met us and she became my full-time sitter. I would club and party Thursday through Saturday, but Ms. Darlene would keep Jhmyra whenever I needed her.

I enrolled back in college and was messing up: barely attending, not doing assignments; shoot, I just didn't care! At this point in my life, I was enjoying myself. I would meet men and tell them lies just to get their money. Once I got their money, I didn't want anything to do with them. I enjoyed telling guys what they wanted to hear. I never gave out my real phone number or address. I was a female player that got what I wanted and didn't give away anything but the radio station phone number. This was hilarious to me.

One day I went to get my hair done at this beauty shop I had been attending for years. I went over to talk to one of the other stylists and there was a guy standing on the side of her. He was wearing a snap back, timberland boots and the fragrance Dolce and Gabbana Light Blue. "A potential candidate," I thought to myself. He was staring at me as if he wanted to say something. But I wasn't going to say anything first; I was going to wait for him. Nevertheless, he never said anything.

The next day, I saw the young lady that I was talking to in the salon at the grocery store. "Tiffany!" she yelled. "I have something to tell you," she said smiling, as if she had the best-kept secret. "The guy that I was talking to in the shop yesterday asked about you."

"For real?" I asked.

"Yes," she said. "He has a good job and he hustles on the side." My eyes lit up like a Christmas tree.

"Jackpot!" I thought to myself. She gave me his number and said to call him. Then she mentioned that he had a girlfriend. "I got this," I confidently said to her, flipping my freshly relaxed hair out of my face.

One Friday night I called him and we talked on the phone for a while. Then I asked if he wanted to meet and talk, and he agreed. We met in the parking lot on Macon Road and was just having a casual conversation, when he suddenly asked, "What type of clothes do you like?" I told him I liked anything that was nice and expensive. He reached into his pocket and pulled out a stack of one hundred-dollar bills and handed me $200. "Now this is my type of guy," I thought to myself. On the next day following our initial meeting, he called me and I invited him over to my house. We sat on the couch and began learning about each other. Unfortunately, he only bragged about himself the entire time. The more he talked, the more I didn't like him.

As days went by, we hardly went anywhere together. I was okay with that, because he had money and I didn't have to do anything to get it. One night he came over and I was still trying to play hard to get; remember, I was the player. We went in my room to watch television, the lights were out and we both laid in the bed side by side, close together. "I really don't like him," I thought. Since he had a friend already, I told myself, "Just get his money."

One Saturday evening, he came over and we went out for hot wings at American Deli restaurant. We sat down to eat and began to converse about his lifestyle. He told me that he was a drug dealer and that he wasn't scared. When I asked him why he was not afraid, he stated that he didn't mind taking a chance to make sure his family was provided for. I really didn't know much about drug dealing so I paid little attention about what he was saying. To me it was just having small talk.

We got back to my place and I tried to throw a hint that I wanted him to leave. It was time for a night out with my girlfriends since it had been a few months since I had seen them. As I started to get dressed, he asked, "Where do you think you're going?"

"Out with my friends that I never get to see," I said rolling my eyes.

"No, you're not," he angrily responded.

"Excuse me?" I said confused. Well from there, he became aggressive and hostile. I was nervous about what could be next, so I decided to stay home.

I started thinking to myself, "This is not right; this man is controlling." He began to spend a lot of time at my house; I didn't have any space! I didn't want to be serious with him; we only had one thing in common which was we both liked nice things. He had lots of money and I didn't have to do much to get what I wanted or needed so I convinced myself to just enjoy things while it lasted.

Every Wednesday I had $150 to pamper myself. I had access to $300 per week to get whatever I needed for my daughter and myself. My friend was always buying gifts for us. I had several designer Coach Bags, designer fragrances, took lavish trips, expensive dinner dates and much more. I was enjoying all the perks of another woman's man. I didn't ever have the intention on being his girlfriend. I only wanted his money.

My friend wanted me to move into a bigger place. But I told him that my apartment was fine and that I didn't want to move. Yet, the more gifts and money he gave me, the more I was convinced to get a place with him. So, we decided to move into a nice townhouse in North Columbus. Actually, I was starting to feel excited about the upgrade! But a few months into the new place, I started to notice a change; he became distant and he would always find a reason to get mad at me so he could stay out late.

On a Friday night, my friend came home looking very angry. I asked if we could go out for dinner, he immediately yelled, "No; *I'm* going out tonight!"

"Why you didn't let me know?" I asked softly.

"I pay all the bills in this house; therefore, if I want to go out, I will," he coldly said. As I tried to hug him and calm him down, he slapped me in the face. I couldn't do anything but cry. He got dressed and left the house.

The next morning, I didn't say anything to him. He was silent as well. I wanted to tell my mom, but I knew she would be upset. My mom was against the move-in with my friend and she told me I was making the wrong choice. I assured her that I would be okay, so I decided to move forward with my plans.

A week passed before my friend and I started to speak again. I really didn't know what to say to him. I was waiting on an apology and never received one. I was ready to end things with my friend and just move on, but I didn't want to lose the benefits. I didn't know what to do. I was sitting in the salon waiting to get my hair done, and my phone rang. It was my boyfriend. He told me to be ready by 7:00 pm so we could go out. I started to smile again and forgot about the altercation.

We went out for dinner and shopping. Later, when we arrived home, he left. Even though I thought we would spend the rest of the evening together. My boyfriend never wanted to be intimate when I wanted to. This behavior from him caused me to have low self-esteem and lack of confidence. He made me feel unwanted and finally, I wanted out of this relationship.

No temptation has overtaken you except what is common to mankind. And God is faithful; he will not let you be tempted beyond what you can bear. But when you are tempted, he will also provide a way out so that you can endure it.

1 Corinthians 10:13

Chapter 4

Distraction from The Past

S itting under the dryer at my usual pampering appointment, I noticed a handsome man walking to the door. I was able to get a good look without him noticing me; there stood my old crush. "Bryan!" I said smiling.

"How have you been?" he asked. I told him all about my situation and how I wanted out of my relationship. After my appointment, we decided to go to a park to finish our conversation.

Bryan asked how I allowed myself to get in such an abusive relationship. I told him things started off alright but later things got worse. Bryan asked if I wanted to spend time with him later and I accepted the offer. I went home, packed a bag, called my friend and headed for her house. I wanted her to have the address of where I would be and headed to meet Bryan. Full of happiness, I pulled up at the hotel and jumped right out of the car without paying attention.

Brian was everything I wanted my boyfriend to be. Bryan made me feel wanted; he listened to me and he always was concerned about my safety. Midnight was approaching and I decided to stay with Bryan. I melted in his arms and our evening ended with passion. I woke up to a light knock on the door, but I ignored it. I was starting to get a weird feeling that something was about to happen. I grabbed my phone and noticed I had more than 60 missed calls from my abusive boyfriend.

Leaving the hotel, I was approaching my car. Suddenly, the door opened and my boyfriend jumped out. Yelling and screaming, he grabbed me by the arm and threw me inside the car. I forgot all about Bryan. I began to cry and panic. My boyfriend was so angry that every question he asked me, I didn't get a chance to respond because he kept slapping me.

We arrived at home and my boyfriend was still angry. I told him none of this would have happed if he was a better boyfriend. Surprisingly, he began to cry. Once I broke away from him, I ran to the restaurant next door and called 911. The police arrived and I told them what happened. Without hesitation, they took my boyfriend to jail.

My boyfriend stayed in jail for the weekend and he made bond. I did not want him back, but I didn't want to lose my perks of being with him. My boyfriend bought me a promise ring so I decided to forgive him for the incident and move on. His behavior changed for a while but he started back acting like his old self. "It's time for a break," I thought to myself.

My brothers and I decided to visit my father in North Carolina; I needed some mental space. My boyfriend was very strange while I was away and we hardly talked on the phone. I was discerning something; like another woman being in the picture. I received a picture from my boyfriend via text message. Something spoke to me and said, "*Scroll all the way down.*" There was another phone number attached to the picture. I called the number and it was another woman.

After arriving home from visiting my dad, I asked my boyfriend if he recognized the number that was attached to the photo he sent me. He said he had never seen the number before. His facial expression confirmed he was lying to me. Later, I noticed I was missing a few birth control pills so I decided to take a test and it was positive. "How could I be pregnant?" I thought. I didn't want a baby by my boyfriend; I wanted to have an abortion.

One day, my boyfriend over heard a conversation I was having on the phone with my girlfriend. I was explaining to her that I was pregnant and that I wanted her to take me to have an abortion. My boyfriend came upstairs and just stood and looked at me. He asked if I was pregnant and I told him yes. I wasn't concerned about him giving me the money for the abortion; for this, I had my own.

Eventually, I decided to call the number back that was attached to the photo my boyfriend sent. The voice of a female said, "Hello," but I immediately hung up. My boyfriend was always staying out late and was very private with his cellular phones. So, I started to pay attention to his actions more. Unfortunately, there were lots of clues that he was seeing another woman. A few weeks went by and I decided that I was going to keep my baby and separate from my boyfriend.

"I want out of this relationship," I stated to him. We argued for a while but didn't conclude one way or the other. The more we argued, the angrier he became. He asked for his money out of the bank, but I told him I was keeping it. In a roar of anger, he punched a hole in the wall. I tried to run downstairs, but my boyfriend grabbed me, yelling, and calling me out of my name. With no control, I was pushed down the stairs. I started to scream and he kicked me. Thank God, I managed to get away to call 911.

My boyfriend was arrested and could not make bail. After that, I really didn't want him back in my life. I didn't want him in my daughter's life either. I decided to ignore him for the first couple of weeks. But after the third week, I began to miss him and started accepting his calls. He told me where he was hiding money in the house and who to hire as his attorney.

I hired a criminal defense lawyer and was told that my boyfriend was going to sit in jail for 45 days. When my boyfriend came home this time, his behavior was worse. We moved into a new place to erase bad memories from the past. On May 8, 2005 I gave birth to a healthy baby girl and we named her Saaniya Jakerra Sneed. I thought that having my daughter would change my boyfriend but it didn't. Money slowed down a lot for my boyfriend in the streets so he decided to pick up extra wor-k painting with his father and I decided to work for my mom.

One day while at work, I received a phone call from the hospital. My boyfriend had been involved in an accident. I rushed to be by his side only to find out he had fallen from a ladder and broken his arm. I begin to cry and I blamed myself for not being there when he cried out for help. My boyfriend was taken into surgery and kept overnight for observation.

I went home to gather some things for my boyfriend, so he could be discharged from the hospital. Driving home, I cried the entire time. Something had my heart very heavy. I arrived home and begin to clean. Suddenly, a small voice said, "Pick up the phone." I picked up the phone and there were 60 missed calls from the same number my boyfriend lied about. My heart felt like it had dropped into my hands. I used my boyfriend's password and unlocked the phone.

I was searching for text messages only to find several asking, "Baby, where are you"? I immediately called the number back from our house phone. The young lady answered and identified herself as Lynn. She confirmed everything I needed to know. My heart felt like someone had pushed a dagger inside it. The pain became worse when she told me that she was six months pregnant with my boyfriend's child.

I waited until my boyfriend's mom got him home and left before I confronted him. Every question I asked him he denied. I knew my boyfriend was being dishonest. I made the decision to part ways from my boyfriend. But before I did, God revealed more deceptions to me. My heart couldn't take anymore, so I found an apartment close by my mom and made plans to move out alone.

Saturday morning, my family came over to help me load my things; my boyfriend had no idea what was going on. There wasn't too much my boyfriend could do because his arm was in a cast. While my family was loading the truck, I told my boyfriend I was leaving him and our relationship was over! I left the house and never looked back.

Three weeks passed; my daughters and I were living on our own and we were happy. My ex would try and reach out to me, but I would ignore him. One evening, I called emergency maintenance because of an issue in my apartment; my ex called right after. He wanted to come and pick up our daughter and take her to the park, but I denied him. He kept calling, but I ignored his calls.

Once the maintenance guy arrived, my ex made one call after another. I began to get nervous and I wanted the maintenance guy to leave. As we walked to the door, we heard footsteps running up the stairs. In slow motion, my front door was kicked in by my ex. In his rage, he held both of us at gun point against our will.

Hours went by and we were still being held hostage. He was accusing me of having a relationship with the maintenance guy. I kept trying to convince him that there was nothing going on between us, but he didn't believe me. I begged my ex to let us go. Finally, he allowed the maintenance man to leave. Apparently, there were some drugs put in the maintenance guy's truck by my ex-boyfriend and a police officer was in on my ex's plans. So, if the cops at the entrance of the apartment complex stopped the maintenance man, the cop knew to search the truck for drugs. When he let the maintenance man leave, I knew I was left alone in the apartment to die. I started to cry.

My ex kept begging for us to get back together, so I agreed because he still had the gun in his hand. He made me have sex with him and he wanted me to promise that I wouldn't call the cops on him. This was the scariest situation I had ever experienced in my life. I managed to pull myself together and got dressed for work.

When I arrived at work, I explained to my mom what had happened. She encouraged me to call the police and file a report, so I did. I didn't feel like working so I decided to leave and go home for the day. My mom was afraid for me to go home alone but I assured her that I would be okay. When I arrived home, I accidently locked my keys in the car. I called a locksmith and as I was giving him my information, I heard a gunshot. My ex-boyfriend had shot the door handle off!

I started screaming to the top of my lungs! My ex slammed me against the wall, took my cell phone and broke it in half. With a gun in my mouth, my ex said to me, "If the police come, I will kill us both!" Crying silently, tears ran down my face. I was mute the entire time; I was too scared to do anything. My house phone rung and he smashed the phone into the fireplace with his foot. There was a knock on the door; we didn't answer.

Then, my ex took my couches and barricaded them against the door. The door knocking became more aggressive. When I looked out of the window, I saw about six police cars in front of my house. An officer kept knocking and trying to get my ex to surrender. I finally managed to get the gun away from my ex. I took the gun and threw it into the freezer. I ran in the back bedroom and started to beat on the window, yelling for help.

I couldn't get the window to open so I ran back to the front room, trying to convince my ex to just surrender. On the other side of the door, a police officer yelled, "Ma'am, step away from the door!" When I moved away from the door and my boyfriend removed his hand from the door, the officer burst into the apartment, threw my ex on the floor and arrested him. He was sentenced to ten years in prison, but served only five. A couple of years after he was released, he only visited our daughter twice. For over a year, no one knew of his whereabouts. Then I heard that he died of a massive heart attack. I could not mourn because my daughter and I were ignored by him for such a long period of time, as well as suffered physical and mental abuse from him. I only hoped that he made peace with God.

But if ye will not do so, behold, ye have sinned against the Lord: and be sure your sin will find you out.

Numbers 32:23 (KJV)

Chapter 5

The Distraction of Money

I didn't want to live in my apartment anymore after the horrible experience I had. I decided to live with my mom for a while until I felt comfortable to live alone again. I used my time wisely by reading books and learning more about myself. *The Things That Steal Your Joy* was the first book I read by Joyce Meyer. I was able to figure out why a lot of things happened in my life while reading this book.

I based my happiness around how other people felt and viewed me. I always wanted to be like other people and I was scared to make life decisions on my own. In spring of 2006, I went back to work and enrolled in school. I was going to try the nursing program one more time. So, I enrolled in Columbus Technical College. Things were going well until I decided I was getting bored.

One day during lunch, I decided to go inside Chick-Fil-A. I saw a handsome dark-skinned guy leaving so I decided to give the cashier my number to give to him. I was expecting a phone call immediately but never received one. Eventually, I forgot about him. I moved back into my own apartment and promised myself I would remain focused and not worry about any guy friends.

One day while leaving my mother's daycare, my phone rang. I didn't recognize the number, so I didn't answer. The number called again, but this time, I answered softly. "Is this Tiffany?" a man said in a deep voice. "Yes," I said blushing. He identified himself and we began sharing our similarities. We made plans to meet in person. Again, I was excited!

Meeting Ramen was not what I expected. He was not that attractive, but his personality was unique. He had his own music group that he was pursuing and he was very smart. I told him I didn't want anything serious with anyone; just a good friend to hang out with and share fun times. Ramen told me his lifestyle didn't allow him to be in a relationship because he was always busy and didn't have much free time.

School was draining and getting the best of me. I was working part-time at the hospital and partying on the weekend. I would spend time with my friend when he was in town. I was enjoying the distance between us because I still had time to hang out with other friends and meet other people. One day, I caught Ramen in a lie. My entire perspective changed towards him, but Ramen was loaded with lots of money so I decided not to confront him.

Ramen would come over, hide money in my purse and pay the majority of my monthly bills. I really didn't want for anything. I decided to quit my job and just focus on school. Two years had gone by and I was in so deep with Ramen. We were not in a committed relationship, but I respected him like we were because he was paying all my bills. I had another guy friend name Nate, but Ramen didn't have a clue.

Nate was in the military and was so handsome, but Nate could not provide for me like Ramen, so I just had fun with them both. At the beginning of the third year with Ramen, I was starting to feel like a sex slave. Ramen had introduced me to things that I had never done before. I found myself doing whatever he would tell me to. Ramen was picky though; I always had to have a fresh pedicure or Ramen didn't want to see me. I was up to getting $500 per week from Ramen, along with any expenses and pleasures that I wanted for me and my girls.

Having a committed relationship with Ramen was not an option. I only wanted his money without the feelings, but I was caught up. The more I would catch him in lies, the more distant I would become. The more distance, the less money I received. Finally, I received a letter in the mail saying that I was being withdrawn from school due to the lack of attendance. I was very disappointed in myself, but I was caught up with the greed for money that I had developed since I met Ramen.

"I need a change," I thought to myself. I called my dad in North Carolina and told him I needed a vacation from Columbus. My dad recommended for me and the girls to move to Raleigh. This is not a bad idea I pondered. November 2006, I went to North Carolina to visit my dad and found a nice spacious loft. I didn't tell any of my family what my plans were because I knew they would try and talk me out of making my transition. In years past, my mother made my brothers and I feel like my father didn't want to have a relationship with us.

May of 2007, I told my mom my decision about relocating for a new start. She was not happy at all. I waivered back and forth about my decision but my heart was set on moving to Raleigh. I had a face to face conversation with my friend about moving and he was not disappointed. Ramen acted as if he didn't care. I was expecting him to beg me to stay, but his reactions made my decision final about moving.

The date was approaching for my girls and me to leave. I needed $350 to move into my loft. "If it's meant for me to move I will get the money," I thought. As time passed, the more excited I became. Before I quit my job, I met a sweet young lady named Tammy. We were experiencing some of the same life issues. Tammy knew I was moving to Raleigh, but I mentioned to her that I couldn't leave because I didn't have the money. Tammy volunteered and gave me $800 and told me that I didn't have to pay her back; this was my sign to leave Columbus, Georgia.

June 5, 2007 my father arrived in Columbus and took my furniture to Raleigh. I decided to stay until June 7th to spend more time with Ramen before I left. My mom finally accepted that I was leaving and decided to give me money for traveling expenses. My daughters and I loaded up my Sonata and left Columbus, Georgia.

For what shall it profit a man, if he shall gain the whole world, and lose his soul?

Mark 8:36

Chapter 6

The Distraction of Deceit

We made it to Raleigh late in the evening. My dad met the girls and I at our new loft to help us get settled in. My dad took us grocery shopping and made us feel very welcomed. The girls and I were so excited we stayed up all night unpacking boxes and organizing our loft. I spoke to Ramen to let him know that we were safe but he was very nonchalant about my newfound happiness. One week went by and I didn't hear anything from my dad. I began to feel that what my mother was telling me was true.

My communication and visits from my dad were very minimal. This made me sad but I managed not to let this hinder me from establishing a relationship with my dad. Ramen and I would talk on the phone every day and night. He asked if I would come down for a weekend to see him and that he would pay for the expenses. I agreed and left the following weekend.

Ramen only wanted to see me if my hair, nails, and toes were done. I dropped my kids off with my mom and went to get pampered. Ramen would always tell me how much he loved me, but he had a weird way of showing me. I was getting tired of meeting up for casual sex; I wanted more than he was ready to give me. On my last day visiting my friend, he asked if I would come over and clean his house and that he would pay me $200. When I arrived at his home, he told me what to do, then he left me there alone.

I began to have weird thoughts that made me feel very sad and alone. I kept cleaning and pondering. Eventually, I decided to go through my friend's things. In my snooping, I found a picture of him with a woman hugging in a night club. I decided not to confront him; I just wanted him out of my life. I left before my friend, Ramen was scheduled to come back home.

Ramen was calling and texting, but I didn't answer. I ignored him the entire night. The next morning, I prepared myself to return to Raleigh. I drove by Ramen's house and noticed a mint green car parked in front of his car. I didn't try to call and ask Ramen any questions. I decided that I deserved someone better and that I wasn't going to have any more connections with Ramen.

Things were not moving as fast as I hoped for in Raleigh. I didn't have a job and I was living off $98 per week. My dad was paying my rent and my mom paid my cell phone bill. I was receiving food and medical assistance, but I didn't have anything extra left over for pleasure. It was tough being in a totally strange place. I wanted a better life for me and my girls, so I knew there would be sacrifices.

I joined a gym right by my house to have something fun to do. I started taking fitness classes and lifting weights. I began loving the way my body started to look. One of the fitness instructors recommended that I apply for a trainer position. So, I did and was offered a job as a personal trainer. They had a child care center and I was able to bring my kids there for free. I was so stoked! On the weekends, I was a server at Applebee's and my dad would watch the girls.

Later, I decided to apply for childcare assistance. The waiting list was one-two years long, but I was approved six months later. Things began to turn for the worse. I arrived home one evening and discovered my lights were disconnected. But God made a way and they came back on two hours later. But the next day I received a letter notifying me that I couldn't renew my lease. I was given thirty days to find my kids and I a new place to live.

I was blessed to find a new townhouse in my price range, but it wasn't going to be ready until two weeks after my 30 days were up in the loft. I begged for more time, but I was denied. My kids and I were homeless for two weeks. I asked my dad if the kids and I could stay with him until my place was ready, but he said his wife didn't approve. I thought about returning to Georgia for two weeks, but I couldn't because of school.

I explained to my mom what happened and told her that I needed a place to live. I found a hotel by my daughter's school and my mom paid for our stay.

Living in the hotel was the most awful experience ever. I couldn't cook, had to go back and forth to the storage unit for clothes and my money was getting low. I only could afford canned meals, box pizza and noodles. Often, we ate Wendy's hamburgers since it was so close.

On the day of our move, I received a call from the apartment manager. I was told that the two- bedroom townhouse was unavailable; I felt helpless. The manager looked at me and said, "We are going to offer you a three bedroom for the same price and its available now!" I immediately embraced her and my heart was filled with joy. Being homeless paid off.

Finally, things were falling into place for the kids and I. Working as a personal trainer was going well for me too. I had a good cliental base and I was happy. August of 2007, I decided that I wanted to enroll in college to study Physical Education. This time I made a promise to myself that I would finish. I met a student advisor on St. Augustine's campus and started school for the fall session.

My sophomore year into college was going great. I made the Dean's list every semester and I was focused like never before. Two days per week, I had a long break in between classes so I decided to go grocery shopping. Wal-Mart was my favorite place to shop because the prices were so good. "Excuse me; are you from here?" a man asked.

"Why?" I asked. Standing in front of me was a light-skinned handsome male wearing a uniform.

He was so attractive in my eyes. We stood and talked in the store for a half hour before we decided to exchange numbers. I received a phone call from the guy I met in the store as soon as I got in the car. He identified himself as Casper. We really didn't have much in common, but he was very smart and spoke really well. Casper was employed with Time Warner cable and was in ministry as a Pastor. "I am not trying to be a first lady," I said to myself.

Casper and I had interesting conversations on the phone. He invited me to lunch one day and I accepted the invitation. He mostly did a lot of talking about himself and the things he had experienced in his past. The more I listened, the more his stories didn't make sense. Valentine's Day was approaching and I was waiting on Casper to ask me out. He was scheduled to have oral surgery the day before. I volunteered to be his driver, so I stayed with him through his entire surgery.

I wasn't expecting for Casper and I to go out on Valentine's Day because of his surgery. Instead, we decided to have a casual get-together at my place. I got off work and rushed home to get ready for Casper. He came over and greeted me with a pink rose, a small box of chocolate and a card. "How sweet!" I thought to myself. The smell of his cologne and his neatly trimmed beard with Beijing was such a turn on. We sat down and enjoyed a glass of wine accompanied by enjoyable conversation.

Casper was like candy to my eyes. I anticipated every house visit and phone call. We were spending a lot of time together. I changed my work schedule on the weekends, so I could be alone with him. Two months into spending time with Casper, I was feeling unsure about his identity. He was too good to be true, and I wanted to know more about him.

One day I was leaving my apartment and saw a friendly police officer. I walked over introduced myself and we started talking about the neighborhood I lived in and Wake County school system. I felt comfortable enough to ask the officer if he could do a background check on someone for me and he did. The officer told me that it would take about two days to come back. Casper and I continued to spend time with each other, but some things weren't adding up.

When I met Casper, he told me that he had two children, had been divorced for seven years and was having a large home built in North Raleigh. I thought to myself, "Why would this successful man want a younger woman with two kids who hasn't finished college yet?" I had nothing to offer Casper but a genuine and authentic heart. A week later, I received a text from the officer about the background check that I requested.

Casper had several addresses, a history for writing worthless checks and a large balance of unpaid child support. "How could you be in the process of owning a home with arrears?" I pondered. I didn't ask Casper anything about what I found out; instead I decided to not worry about his past and focus on his future. Casper had a smooth way of making things sound so compelling and truthful. As time went on, I forgot all about what the officer told me.

Three months later, I found out I was pregnant. I was so nervous and scared. I wasn't ready for another child. I wanted to be married and finish with college. I didn't want to tell Casper about the pregnancy; I wanted an abortion. I told my mom the news and we agreed that having the abortion was the best thing to do. I never really believed in abortions, but I was determined not to have a baby until after marriage.

I told Casper the news and he didn't seem upset, but shocked. I had the abortion a few weeks later and was going to end things with Casper, but I wasn't strong enough to stick to my plans. My flesh was out of control. We started spending more and more time together that mentally, I blocked everything out except Casper. A couple months later, I found out I was pregnant again.

Casper was living with his relative in Knightdale, so we decided to be involved in a relationship and move in together. Casper told me he was deeply committed to his church and because of the calling on his life, he wasn't funding another abortion. I accepted the pregnancy and continued to work and attend college. Casper received a phone call one day from an old friend; he didn't want to answer the phone, so I did. A young lady described herself as a friend of Casper and told me that they had been having a sexual relationship for a while. The young lady also told me that Casper was married with six kids.

My heart felt like it dropped in my hands. I was so hurt and devastated. But of course, Casper denied everything the young lady stated to me. I really wanted to believe him, but I didn't have peace about the situation at all. I tried to let things go but my heart was too heavy. I continued to attend school even though I was very sick. I went to my Professor that I was very close to and told her the news. She asked me who was I pregnant by and I told her. My professor knew Casper and confirmed everything the young lady revealed to me about Casper.

I confronted Casper about everything I found out. Casper denied every accusation that was exposed about him. I didn't believe him. His stories weren't adding up about the kids. Later in my pregnancy, Casper admitted to everything being true that I found out about him. I was so upset and enraged, but there was nothing I could do about it. I didn't want to have my son alone, so I decided to stay and make things work.

Casper promised me that he would provide for us and make sure things were taken care of. Things were okay

42

at times, but Casper was very inconsistent. Feb 1, 2010, I gave birth to a healthy baby boy by another woman's husband. Casper and I decided to move into a bigger place and move forward in our relationship since his divorce had become final. Immediately after moving into our new place, the finances turned for the worse. Casper wasn't bringing in enough money and the IRS had attached a wage garnishment to his employment. Casper never told me about this. It just so happened that the notification letter fell out of his bible as I was cleaning.

I didn't confront Casper about this because there were too many situations I caught him lying about. I was forced to go back to work when my son was only five weeks old. I was determined to graduate on time, so I returned to class when my son was a week old. Day after day the finances got worse. We received eviction letters almost every month, my car was repossessed and the gas was cut off. I begged Casper to get another job, but he wouldn't. I decided to go find another job making more money in my last year of college.

The job I found paid me well, but I was fed up with Casper's inconsistency and lack of responsibility. A month after graduation, I decided to look for another place for me and my kids. I didn't let Casper catch on to anything I was doing. I made all of my moves during the day time while he was working. I managed to find my kids and I a nice apartment and arranged to have our things moved out while Casper was working. One

Saturday evening, Casper came home to an empty apartment.

Casper called me crying but I wasn't moved by his tears. I had been through so much with Casper and it was time for me to let go. I cared deeply for him but not enough to keep being stupid. Living alone again felt good at times but often I was lonely. I missed his presence, but I blocked it out most of the time. Casper and I were separated for a year but remained in a sexual relationship. The entire time were apart, my kids and I never struggled. I was fortunate enough to save $15,000 in my savings account.

On Mother's Day of 2014, I went to church and heard a message that pertained to my relationship with Casper, so I decided that I wanted him back. We made plans to get married in the fall. As we got closer to our wedding day, Casper was not showing any improvement of being consistent for his family. I wanted him to change so badly that I was willing to do whatever it took to help him. We signed up for six weeks of pre-marital counseling and I hoped things would be better.

I applied everything the counselors told me to do but it was hard. We both kept saying things to each other that we were advised not to say. I had always wanted to be married and have my own family, so I just remained quiet and focused on the big day that was approaching. A week before my wedding day, another secret came out about Casper. A voice spoke to me and said, "Don't rush into this." But I ignored the voice and the secret. The day before the wedding, I was given a sign to call off the wedding, but I wanted to be married and I still proceeded with the plans.

My family didn't approve of me marrying Casper. My mom definitely didn't agree. My mom saw straight through Casper from day one. My mom and I argued all time about me being with a man like Casper. I overlooked every sign and experience and said, "I do" on September 6, 2014. The wedding was very nice; a lot of my family came for the wedding, but over half of Casper's family didn't show up. The next morning, we flew to Miami and went on a Western Caribbean cruise.

The second day on the cruise, I woke up crying. I had a feeling that I had made a terrible mistake. Casper asked me what was wrong and I lied to him. I told him that I missed the kids. We got back to Raleigh and I put my notice in to resign from my job. I decided that I wanted to be an entrepreneur in the fitness industry. Casper didn't agree, so two months later I asked Casper to leave. I told him that I could no longer handle the lies and the irresponsible things that he did, such as neglected the rent, depended on me to hustle for the family, and never saved any money. I wanted a divorce.

Casper stayed away from the house for a few months, but we remained sexual. I decided to reconcile because Casper always blamed me for us breaking up. I decided to accept the blame and work on being a better wife. Things began to get better for us: my business was prospering, Casper was making sales, and we became Pastor and First Lady of a church. I was nervous about being a First Lady, but I supported my husband and told him I would stand by his side. I even purchased the basic things we needed for the church: the podium, offering baskets, tithe envelopes, communion cups and I was paying my tithes to my husband, so we could get a church building.

I'd thought my marriage had a better chance of lasting by being in a leadership position, but it didn't. We argued a lot and we could never agree on anything concerning the church. I felt like I was being overlooked. As days passed, we became more distant. All our conversations ending in arguments, I felt like all hope was lost for my marriage. I went to my husband and told him that I had fallen out of love. We agreed that in three months he would move out and that we would file for a divorce.

My husband and I were together a total of seven years. I wanted my marriage to work badly but most of the time I was the only one fighting for it. I had mixed emotions about wanting a divorce but most of all, I wanted peace. I started a part-time job at a local gym as a front desk associate, so I could make up the deficit from my husband's absence.

As days passed, my healing process became easier. I read the Bible every day, fasted and prayed. I started with the book of Genesis by reading three to four chapters daily. The more I read the Bible, the stronger

I became mentally. The more I fasted, the more God revealed to me about my husband. I read the Bible so much it tasted like honey. Every time the devil put negative thoughts in my mind, I turned to the Bible. I surrounded myself with positive people and cut off the negative ones.

One day, I connected with a minister via Facebook. She was always positive and inspiring. I decided to open up to her about what I was going through. She began to explain to me how God was preparing me for ministry and after bonding, Minister Harper became my spiritual mother. The more I received spiritual counseling, the more I saw myself as a strong woman of God. As I continued to build my relationship with God, the distractions still came, but I was more equipped with the armor of God. Because of the Word of God, I have been able to overcome and be victorious in the battle of distractions which were set-up for my destruction.

Put on the full armor of God, so that you can take stand against the devil's schemes.

Ephesians 6:11

Meet the Author

Tiffany Bostic was born in Raleigh, North Carolina and currently resides in Columbus, Georgia. She has a B.S. in Human Performance and Wellness and a mother of three beautiful children. She is a Fitness Coach, empowering people through physical health and wellness, as well as spiritually.

Contact Information for Tiffany:

Email Address: tbostic22@gmail.com

Facebook: Figure Bostic Tiffany MsFit

99892882R00033

Made in the USA
Columbia, SC
14 July 2018